SOLDIERS AND UNIFORMS
OF THE AMERICAN ARMY
1775–1954

Fritz Kredel
Text by Frederick P. Todd

DOVER PUBLICATIONS, INC.
Mineola, New York

Bibliographical Note

This Dover edition, first published in 2005, is an unabridged republication of all the plates and facing descriptions from the revised edition of the work, as originally published by Henry Regnery Company, Chicago, in 1954 under the title *Soldiers of the American Army, 1775–1954.*

Library of Congress Cataloging-in-Publication Data

Kredel, Fritz, 1900–1973.
    [Soldiers of the American Army, 1775–1954]
    Soldiers and uniforms of the American Army, 1775–1954 / Fritz Kredel ; text by Frederick P. Todd.
        p. cm.
    Originally published: Soldiers of the American Army, 1775–1954. Rev. ed. Chicago : H. Regnery Co., 1954.
    Includes bibliographical references.
    ISBN 0-486-44042-7 (pbk.)
    1. United States. Continental Army—Uniforms. 2. United States. Army—Uniforms. I. Todd, Frederick P. II. Title.

UC483.K7 2005
355.1'4'0973—dc22

                        2004061800

Manufactured in the United States of America
Dover Publications, Inc., 31 East 2nd Street, Mineola, N.Y. 11501

Introduction

WHEN THE FIRST edition of this work was published, in 1941, the United States was still at peace. A book about American soldiers, and especially a book which undertook to show how they appeared, was in those years so unusual as to excite considerable comment. In writing the Introduction to the first edition, therefore, it was felt important to explain something of the nature of regimental *esprit de corps*, something about the background of military institutions in this country, and to add an almost apologetic note on the traditional American apathy towards things military.

Since 1941 American arms have fought—and I shall say, helped to win—three wars. Today American garrisons literally encircle the earth. Missions and materiel despatched from the United States are training a dozen countries in the art of fighting on land, sea and air. Whereas a generation ago scarcely one in twenty boys in this country had ever shouldered a rifle, today there are very few young American males who have not received some sort of military training.

It is not possible for a people to undergo such a transformation without beginning to wonder what heritage they possess to meet so vast a martial challenge. In a hundred ways this new curiosity is evident. Artists and writers have begun to dig into military history; private accumulations of military books, pictures, weapons and other objects today rival the more traditional fields of collecting; the Service departments in Washington now maintain historical bureaus of a size and competence unheard of earlier; and the social scientists, who for so long have not only ignored but actually resisted military studies, have launched upon an organized and well financed investigation of civil-military relations in America which promises to bring the subject into its rightful place in the classroom and lecture hall.

In view of this swelling interest a new edition of *Soldiers of the American Army* is easily justified. The original edition has long been out of print and it is well nigh impossible today to secure a copy. High priced because of its hand colored illustrations, the book remained beyond the reach of many who could have made the most use of it. For this reason, the new edition has been produced on as popular a scale as is possible.

The new edition has been considerably revised. In the first place, the final plates of the first edition showed types of soldiers in the experimental kits of 1940 and 1941—kits which were, in some cases, widely revised before our armies entered combat. It was thought desirable to replace these with drawings of the uniforms our troops actually wore in the field and in general to bring the book up to date. This has been done, and the opportunity was enlarged upon to add a few more of the older types of uniforms that played important roles in our military history.

There was still another issue to be met. Increased interest in military history has brought increased knowledge of the minutiae of research. Reference sources unknown in 1941 to the author and artist have been exploited in the past ten years. The body of knowledge on military dress and accoutrements in particular has been enlarged tremendously in this country. Use was made of this new material and every plate of the original edition has been scrutinized and changes made where necessary. In a sense, then, this is as much a new book as a reprint of an older one.

Some of the recently created sources of American military history are listed among the *References* at the end of this work. But there is one with which the artist and author have been especially concerned, because it attempts to show how the American soldier looked, and what he carried, and in which outfits he served. This is the *Company of Military Collectors & Historians*, and to its membership and journal we are greatly indebted for inspiration and practical help in this revision.

*   *   *

When K Battery, First Artillery, undertook a practice march in the summer of 1895, it happened to pass through the streets of Great Barrington, Massachusetts. A local paper pointed out that only twice before had artillery come within the township borders—once in 1776 when Henry Knox hauled the ordnance captured at Fort Ticonderoga through the town on its way to Boston, and the second time when cannon taken from the British at Saratoga were being carted to West Point. The citizens of the town were awed, almost alarmed, at the rattling gun carriages and the trim cannoneers, so unaccustomed were they to the sight of soldiers. Only a few old men—veterans of the Civil War—dared venture near enough to inspect the new breech loaders.

Sixty years have passed since then and still only friendly cannon have rolled through the streets of Great Barrington. But no longer are its citizens awed by the sight of guns and soldiers. The two conditions, in the world of today, are not unrelated; if this book can be said to have a moral, it is that only by knowing about military matters can a people confidently approach the problems of their national protection. The streets of Great Barrington have remained free from enemy cannon chiefly because its citizens have, in some part, become soldiers themselves.

FREDERICK P. TODD

West Point, N. Y.

Introduction to the First Edition

A n army is composed of men, together with a great array of weapons and other paraphernalia of war. Yet these men with all their equipment are not in themselves the army any more than students, faculty, and Gothic architecture make a university. Between the raw materials of an establishment and the establishment itself are the ideas, traditions, and organization which form it into a living force. These, in an army, are called military institutions.

In telling in pictorial form of the soldiers of the American army the story has been told in the framework of these institutions. The accomplishments of a regiment, for example, are often stressed. This is because the regiment of some one thousand men is the ideal unit for bearing these institutions. It is large enough to survive the changes demanded by tactical developments and the losses sustained in battle, yet small enough for its members to know one another and to sense the "touch of elbows," that indefinable feeling of solidarity which is the key to achievement. In the regiment—in good regiments, that is—one finds real *esprit de corps*, which is, after all, the soul of any military unit.

In the pages which follow there will be mentioned the work of individuals, such men as Washington, Steuben, and Thayer. These have been men with ideas, with imagination and rare courage; these are the men who have built our army and have created—sometimes almost from whole cloth—the regiments and the corps portrayed. And the remarkable part about them is that they have built this army and its traditions with little or no help from us Americans. Indeed, it can almost be said that they have built it in spite of us. These men are not pictured in the plates which follow. Instead will be found the soldiers who served under and for them. We feel that they would have liked it better this way.

Some of the types may seem bizarre, but it was not intended to make them so. Their novelty rests in the simple fact that they have never been sketched before. This absence of illustrative material is really remarkable. In the fifty years between 1775 and 1825 the artists of Europe—under all sorts of governments and conditions—produced countless thousands of paintings, sketches, engravings, and statuettes of the soldiery they saw. Yet in that same period, embracing two long wars, the number of real military pictures executed in America can be counted on the fingers of both hands. And most of those were the work of foreigners. We did not lack for artists—for primitive ones at least—and we had plenty of troops under arms. Why were they not pictured?

The reason probably lies deep in the American character. The affection and concern any people hold for their national institutions is reflected to a large degree in the frequency with which these institutions are portrayed in color or stone. Those things which they do not know or like are left unpainted. Let us be charitable then and conclude that we in America have not known our army. If this is true, it is time that we make its acquaintance.

The principal sources of reference used in its preparation are listed toward the rear of this volume, but a few words of explanation and tribute should be added here concerning those works which have been especially helpful. The general studies of our Army by Upton,

Spaulding, and Ganoe are obviously indispensable in a compilation of this kind. Since they relate in one way or another to every plate, they have been cited only at the end. The more specialized works, however, particularly those containing pictorial material, may need some slight introduction.

Between 1839 and 1841 there appeared in the *U. S. Military Magazine* a series of prints which can be said to mark the beginning of American military art. Other examples followed, many of exceptional beauty. The Mexican War brought the battle scenes of Nebel; the Civil War introduced the engravings of Forbes and the photographs of Brady; the Indian Frontier gave us the incomparable Remington. These men drew the soldier as they saw him. Careful and realistic, they stood for the best in martial portraiture.

By the 1890's the field of military illustration was well developed, and a new departure had been made by several men like Howard Pyle and Harry A. Ogden. Combining the arts of the historian with their own, they undertook to draw the soldier as he had existed formerly. In 1886 the Quartermaster General issued Ogden's plates covering the uniforms of the Army since 1775, the first book of its kind in this country. Other work of the same sort followed, notably the drawings of the American Revolution by Charles H. Lefferts, whose detailed studies were cut short by his untimely death.

The productions of these men have lighted the way. Recently the work of H. Charles McBarron, Jr., a splendid military artist, has appeared in several journals. Other students are opening up the rich fields offered by governmental archives. To all of these people of the past and present alike we owe our thanks. Through their accomplishments we have been able to add this small but sincere tribute to the Soldiers of the American Army.

FREDERICK P. TODD

American Military Institute, Washington, D. C.

LIST OF PLATES

PLATE 1. General George Washington

Farewell orders to the Armies of the United States:

¶ ". . . It only remains for the Comdr in Chief to address himself once more, and that for the last time, to the Armies of the U States (however widely dispersed the individuals who compose them may be) and to bid them an affectionate, a long farewell. . . .

"A contemplation of the compleat attainment (at a period earlier than could have been expected) of an object for which we contended against so formidable a power cannot but inspire us with astonishment and gratitude. The disadvantageous circumstances on our part, under which the war was undertaken, can never be forgotten. The singular interpositions of Providence in our feeble condition were such, as could scarcely escape the attention of the most unobserving; while the unparalleled perserverance of the Armies of the U States, through almost every possible suffering and discouragement for the space of eight long years, was little short of a standing miracle.

"It is not the meaning nor within the compass of this address to detail the hardships peculiarly incident to our service, or to describe the distresses, which in several instances have resulted from the extremes of hunger and nakedness, combined with the rigours of an inclement season; nor is it necessary to dwell on the dark side of our past affairs. Every American Officer and Soldier must now console himself, for any unpleasant circumstances which may have occurred by a recollection of the uncommon scenes in which he has been called to Act no inglorious part, and the astonishing events of which he has been a witness, events which have seldom if ever before taken place on the stage of human action, nor can they probably ever happen again. For who has before seen a disciplined Army form'd at once from such raw materials? Who, that was not a witness, could imagine that the most violent local prejudices would cease so soon, and that men who came from the different parts of the Continent, strongly disposed, by the habits of education, to despise and quarrel with each other, would instantly become but one patriotic band of Brothers, or who, that was not on the spot, can trace the steps by which such a wonderful revolution has been effected, and such a glorious period put to all our warlike toils?

"It is universally acknowledged, that the enlarged prospects of happiness, opened by the confirmation of our independence and sovereignty, almost exceeds the power of description. . . .

"To the various branches of the Army the General takes this last and solemn opportunity of professing his inviolable attachment and friendship."

Rock Hill, near Princeton,
November 2, 1783

GENERAL GEORGE WASHINGTON

PLATE 2. Thompson's Pennsylvania Rifle Battalion, 1775

O F ALL the types of soldier which made up the Continental Line—foot, horse, and gunners —the rifleman was the most distinctly American. He was just as distinctive as the frontier from which he came; not because he carried a rifle or wore a buckskin shirt, but rather because he came from a folk whose resourcefulness, tenacity, and vision won an entire continent. Bred to these qualities, the rifleman had a natural dislike of convention which was at once his strength and his weakness. Like the ranger of the Old French War before him, he was ever the irregular, hard to manage, contemptuous of discipline, restless under the inevitable routine of an army, but deadly when properly employed.

Since riflemen could be found only along the western borders of the colonies, they numbered but a few special corps. The most distinguished were those commanded by William Thompson and Samuel Miles of Pennsylvania and by Daniel Morgan of Virginia. The first corps, raised in June and July 1775, was composed of expert riflemen from Pennsylvania, Maryland, and Virginia. It took part in the siege of Boston in that year, and two of its companies accompanied Arnold on his march to Quebec. During the months that followed, the frontiersman were transformed into disciplined, efficient soldiers, and on January 1, 1776, the regiment became the 1st of the Continental Line. When the Line was renumbered the next year, it became the 1st Pennsylvania; as such, its history is the history of the Revolution.

The hunting or rifle shirt in which this corps was clothed is shown in the plate. It was the familiar frontier garment. In its most common form it was made of deerskin for winter and linen for summer, reaching often to the knees and having one or more capes. Being open down the front and without buttons, it had to be held together by a broad leather belt by which was carried a knife or hatchet. The cloth shirts were dyed in a wide variety of shades, but those of skin appear usually to have been of an ash or tan color. This hunting shirt was widely used throughout the entire army by mounted and foot troops alike.

In the course of the war most of the companies of the 1st Pennsylvania turned in their rifles for smoothbore muskets. The rifle, although highly accurate, was difficult to load and unable to carry a bayonet so that it did not measure up as a military weapon. The right figure in the plate is a rifleman; the man on the left is from a company which has been altered to infantry. Both wear the painted canvas knapsacks issued to Pennsylvania units early in the war.

[*Pennsylvania Archives*, 2nd ser., X, 3-42, 305-90; John W. Wright, "Some Notes on the Continental Army," in the *William and Mary College Quarterly*, 2nd ser., XI, 196-98; Charles M. Lefferts, *Uniforms . . . of the American Revolution* (New York, 1926); John G. W. Dillin, *The Kentucky Rifle* (Washington, 1924); colored engraving by Daniel N. Chodowiecki, in *Allgemeines historisches Taschenbuch . . . für 1784 . . .* ; MS Archives of Maryland, Red Book 4, No. 13.]

Musketman

Rifleman

THOMPSON'S PENNSYLVANIA RIFLE BATTALION · 1775

PLATE 3. Baylor's 3rd Continental Dragoons, 1778

THE EASTERN seaboard along which the Revolution was fought was not ideal terrain for cavalry. Nevertheless, there were numerous occasions upon which mounted men were urgently needed but were not available. Late in 1776 Congress authorized four regiments of horse to be called, after the British system, light dragoons. But so great was the difficulty in procuring mounts, equipment, and men that the troops were always far under strength. A cavalryman had to take care of his horse as well as perform all the other tasks of a soldier, and the service, consequently, was not overly popular. One state cavalry regiment had enlisted its men on the promise of exemption from menial tasks, but Washington wisely declined its services on the grounds of impartiality and discipline.

Then, too, care had to be taken to enlist in the dragoons only native Americans of known stability and proven loyalty. This was a practice in all armies of that day, for the horsemen were often called upon to act as military police. So it was that the dragoons became an elite corps, and no unit was more so than Colonel George Baylor's 3rd Regiment, the "Lady Washington Dragoons." Raised in 1777, it served throughout the war. Its officers and men came principally from the horse raising districts of Virginia and Maryland, although at least one troop was formed in Pennsylvania. Its personnel were, therefore, born horsemen.

During much of 1777 and 1778 Baylor's Dragoons furnished details to the Commander-in-Chief's Guard. The Guard itself was an infantry unit of picked men stationed permanently at headquarters, and the attached dragoons served as patrols, videttes, and couriers, as escort for Washington and his staff, and as guards of honor to distinguished visitors.

The light dragoon regiments wore distinctive uniforms when they could get them. The 1st used blue faced with red, or brown faced with green; the 2nd, blue faced with buff; the 3rd, white faced with light blue; and the 4th, red faced with blue, and later green faced with red. As shown in the plate, they were armed with heavy sabres and flint-lock pistols, the latter carried in holsters hanging from the pommel of the saddle. When procurable, they carried carbines as well, but these weapons were so extremely scarce that cavalry were often unable to protect their own camps from enemy attack. The 3rd Dragoons was almost annihilated near Hackensack in September 1778 when its post was attacked in the night by a British force under Major General Charles Grey—"No-Flint Grey" of Paoli notoriety. But the regiment recovered and under Colonel William Washington played a gallant part in the Southern campaigns where it was pitted against such vigorous foemen as Tarleton's Legion.

[Wright, op. cit., 189-92; Lefferts, op. cit.; Carlos E. Godfrey, The Commander-in-Chief's Guard (Washington, 1904); colored engraving by Daniel N. Chodowiecki, in Allgemeines historisches Taschenbuch . . . für 1784 . . . ; portrait of Lt. Col. William Washington in the Maryland Historical Society.]

BAYLOR'S 3rd CONTINENTAL DRAGOONS

TROOPERS SERVING AS CAVALRY OF THE COMMANDER·IN·CHIEF'S GUARD · 1778

PLATE 4. "Congress' Own" and the Continental Artillery, 1780

MOST OF the regiments of the Continental Army were named and numbered for the states from which they came. Although Washington strove for a national army, he soon discovered that troops from the different states would not mix. By stressing the state spirit within the regiments, he thus turned this jealousy to advantage.

Certain units, however, were drawn from the country at large, and one of these, the 2nd Canadian Regiment, "Congress' Own," is of particular interest. It was raised early in 1776, partly in Canada and from among Canadian refugees, the rest from various states. Its commander was Moses Hazen, a vigorous and independent soldier who had won his spurs as an officer of rangers in the Old French War and had later held the King's commission. The regiment fought through part of the Northern campaign, saw action on numerous fields including Brandywine, Germantown, and Yorktown. From the first to last it was counted a splendid command.

The officer shown is the captain of a light company, as is indicated by the leather cap worn in place of the cocked hat. He is in the dress uniform of the regiment, brown faced with red. Although his subaltern officers sometimes carried light muskets, he himself is shown with an espontoon, the weapon with which he was armed both on parade and in battle. This was a doctrine laid down by Baron Steuben; an officer busy shooting his musket was not much good as a leader.

The Artillery was also drawn from the country at large. This important branch, comprising four fine regiments and several auxiliary units, was almost entirely the outgrowth of a Volunteer artillery company called "The Train," formed in Boston in 1763. Here such leading artillerymen as Henry Knox, John Crane, and Winthrop Sargent obtained their first training in arms.

The soldier shown here is a gunner. It was his duty to load the piece and, after each shot, to swab the bore with the wet sponge he holds in his right hand lest a spark remain to explode the next charge. He also carries a drag rope which, fastened to hooks on the carriage, aided him in moving the piece. His uniform of dark blue or black, faced with red, was one of the most common of the Revolution and was regularized for the Artillery in 1779. His long overalls—a most practical garment for service on this Continent—had by 1780 become the popular form of leg covering. Like the rifle shirt, it was worn by all arms and ranks.

Both of the men in the plate make a smart appearance. The white ribbons on their black cockades indicate the French alliance and the consequent improvement in supplies, but this alone was not the reason for their smartness. To understand it one must look back to that winter at Valley Forge when Steuben had made over the Continental Army.

[Lefferts, *op. cit.; Pennsylvania Archives*, 1st ser., VIII, 17-20; John Muller, *A Treatise of Artillery . . .* (Philadelphia, 1779); Francis S. Drake, *Life and Correspondence of Henry Knox* (New York, 1873) 14, 21.]

Artillery gunner   *Captain of a light company, 2nd Canadian Regiment*

"CONGRESS' OWN" AND THE CONTINENTAL ARTILLERY · 1780

PLATE 5. Infantry of the Legion, 1795

In the peace which followed the Revolution the Regular Army was reduced to less than a hundred men and no adequate provision was made for using the Volunteer corps of the different states. Instead, reliance was placed on the common militia to curb the growing Indian troubles along our vast and savage frontier. It was no more useful in this instance than it has been at other times, and after the severe defeats of 1790 and 1791 a regular force of some size was raised and placed under the command of General Anthony Wayne.

Wayne was an active, capable officer, and under his strong leadership the new, raw force was whipped into an excellently disciplined and trained command. It was reorganized into what was called the Legion, divided into four sublegions. Each sublegion was a complete fighting unit in itself, with its proportion of infantry, rifles, cavalry, and artillery. With these troops he moved west in 1793 to near what is now Cincinnati, and next year decisively beat the Indians at Fallen Timbers on the Maumee River. The forts built by Wayne in this campaign marked the military frontier. Far in advance of the settlements ran this protecting cordon of tiny posts, ever moving ahead as the American nation began its westward progress. Thus commenced the Army's long duty of guarding the frontier.

The Infantry of the Legion wore the blue coat faced with red which by then was almost a national uniform. For headdress they wore a leather cap or ordinary round hat trimmed with a roach of bear skin, cloth band, cockade, and feather. By orders of September 11, 1792, the men of the 1st Sublegion wore caps with black hair, white band and plume; those of the 2nd Sublegion, white hair, red band and plume; those of the 3rd, black hair, yellow band and plume; and those of the 4th, white hair, green band and plume. Company officers on duty wore the same hats as their men; field officers used the style of cocked hat then in fashion, with the sublegion feather.

This, the uniform worn on parade and the "grand guards," is shown in the plate. On such occasions the hair was carefully dressed and powdered, the white belts were pipe-clayed, and the brass polished until it sparkled—Wayne knew the value of smartness. So garbed, the Legion paraded over the chip-strewn drill yards to impress visiting Indian chiefs and improve its own morale. But, when it left the log stockades and moved out along the Indian war trails, its men were once more garbed in the fringed hunting jacket of the West.

[Manuscript dress regulations in The National Archives; "General Wayne's Orderly Book, 1792-1797" in Michigan Pioneer and Historical Society *Collections*, XXXIV (1904), 346-733; Thomas Boyd, *Mad Anthony Wayne* (New York, 1931).]

Captain of the 2nd Sublegion   *Private of the 1st Sublegion*

INFANTRY OF THE LEGION · 1795

PLATE 6. The Regiment of Artillerists, 1812

Paramount among the "Old Corps" of the Army at the outbreak of the second war with Great Britain was the Regiment of Artillerists. Indeed, it was the oldest corps, descended in direct line from Alexander Hamilton's New York Artillery Company, raised in 1776. Able men like John Doughty, Henry Burbeck, Stephen Rochefontaine, and Louis Toussard had served as its commandants. For many years it had been closely associated with the Corps of Engineers and the new Military Academy at West Point. By 1812, therefore, it was a model for all the elite Volunteer artillery being formed in the larger cities, even to the copying of its uniform and the use of the drill manuals written by its officers.

Artillery of this sort was called "foot artillery," since it served as both infantry and cannoneers. Its iron guns, heavy six- or twelve-pounders, were drawn by hired teams with civilian drivers, the men marching along side. It was slow work and for some time progressive officers had advocated the newer "horse artillery," then being exploited by Napoleon, in which every man was mounted. But not until the alarm occasioned by the "Chesapeake affair" of 1807 was a regiment of this sort authorized, and it was still many, many years before our artillery was permanently and properly mounted.

The Regiment of Artillerists at this time, as befitted their veteran standing, wore the chapeau bras or cocked hat and the long tailed coat reminiscent of the previous century. These are shown on both soldiers in the plate. Other units had by then adopted the shako and short tails, popularized by the French armies and symbolic of the new revolutionary order, but the Artillerists, like Napoleon's Old Guard, retained the more traditional forms. Only the use of buttons instead of hooks and the straight front to the coat are "modern."

The drummer was clad in red, faced with blue—the reverse of the other men—so that he might be located readily in battle to sound the calls. In the clothing shortages which came with the War of 1812 captured British coats were put to good use in clothing these musicians.

[Manuscript dress regulations and orders in The National Archives; Louis De Toussard, *American Artillerist's Companion* (Philadelphia, 1809); William E. Birkhimer, *Historical Sketch . . . of the Artillery, United States Army* (Washington, 1884).]

Matross and drummer, parade uniform

THE REGIMENT OF ARTILLERISTS · 1812

PLATE 7. Regular Infantry, 1814

CONTRASTING sharply with the older units of the regular "peace establishment" were the new regiments raised hastily in 1812 and 1813 to meet the emergencies of the second war with Great Britain. Although nominally Regulars, they were at first no better than the state militias which were called out at the same time. In these years thirty-seven infantry regiments alone were established, but none of them could then be adequately manned, officered, or trained. So great was the ignorance, confusion, and apathy of both country and Army that by July 1812 only 6,686 men were under arms in a force authorized at 35,603.

The chaos was equally great in the supply departments. It was found impossible to equip and arm the new units adequately even though they were far below strength, and months before the war began the shortage of blue cloth forced the Purveyor of Public Supplies to resort to substitute uniforms of various sorts. Clothes of grey, brown, and drab mixtures were hastily made up and issued. Facings were omitted or simplified, and an attempt to send the same makeshifts to a single regiment was the only effort toward uniformity.

The figures in the plate reflect this discord. The sergeant on the left is dressed in a grey "roundabout" jacket and trousers, designed for drill and fatigue but more often worn for all purposes. His white epaulettes and red sash indicate his grade. The private of the 6th wears a regulation infantry "coatee" with fatigue trousers of brown linen. Both men have short pantaloons, although the older style of overalls with tongues and straps—shown on the Legion soldier in plate no. 4—was still widely worn in the Army.

Both men wear the leather cap adopted for foot troops in 1813. Its high front rendered it very similar to the type used by the British. The flap behind could be let down to protect the neck. For decoration it had a metal plate, a leather cockade with a brass eagle, a tasselled cord, and a felt pompon on the left side. The 6th Infantry was permitted to wear a buck's tail in place of the pompon, a custom also observed by some Volunteers and in the Marine Corps.

By 1814 some order had been brought to the agencies of supply, and the clothing regained a fair amount of its martial appearance. But more important than this, the men themselves, under the leadership and hard training of vigorous officers like Winfield Scott, began to gain a new confidence. On July 5, still clad in the rough grey kersey, this infantry of Scott's met and trounced the British at Chippewa. The grey uniform became a proud symbol, and it has long been maintained that this episode led to its adoption for the cadets of the Military Academy. Certainly it became a familiar military dress in America thereafter.

[Manuscript orders and regulations in The National Archives; H. Charles McBarron, Jr., "American Military Dress in the War of 1812. III. Regular Infantry," in *Journal* of the American Military Institute, IV, 185-96; Charles W. Elliott, *Winfield Scott: The Soldier and the Man* (New York, 1937).]

Sergeant, 32nd Regiment

Private, 6th Regiment

REGULAR INFANTRY · 1814

PLATE 8. United States Military Academy, 1825

The United States Military Academy was founded in 1802 through the foresight and wise counsel of such men as Washington, Hamilton, and Knox. Since then it has grown with the Army—in size, accomplishments, and vision. Its record makes it stand out today as perhaps the greatest and most lasting military benefit of the Revolution.

The early management of the Academy was beset with numerous troubles, yet by 1825 the strong, clear-sighted regime of Sylvanus Thayer had taken hold and had established a doctrine of tactical and academic achievement which lasts until our own day. In 1825 there were some 250 cadets in the school. One of them, Robert E. Lee, had just entered; another, Jefferson Davis, was a yearling. Outside the reservation the famed Benny Havens sold his waffles and forbidden liquids; inside the students labored over books and problems very much as they do today. And beneath it all the great Hudson glided ceaselessly by and into the memory of those who watched it.

The cadets of those days wore the familiar grey coat which had been adopted in 1815 or 1816, traditionally in honor of the grey jackets worn by the Regulars at Chippewa. There is every reason to believe this, although it is probable that grey fatigue clothing was not unknown at the Point some years before. Since then the uniform has remained virtually unchanged. White cross belts were worn for infantry drill; black waist belts and a straight sword for other occasions. The cadets were armed with a shorter musket than the infantry, and various other modifications were made in the equipment to suit the boys in their 'teens who made up the Corps.

The Academy has always stressed drill and parades, with the result that the Corps of Cadets has for over a century maintained the reputation of being the best drilled unit in this country and the peer of any of the crack European regiments. This fame is due in no small measure to the Academy Band. It has played its marches and salutes since 1813 when Colonel Alexander Macomb sent his own musicians to West Point from the harbor forts of New York.

In 1825 the Band comprised about twenty experienced musicians, and each cadet was charged a small fee to furnish the extra pay given its members. Their instruments included cymbals, clarinets, hautbois, trumpets, and bassoons, beside the usual drums and fifes; but the new *cornets-à-pistons* had not yet found their way to the Academy. The bandsmen, in keeping with the universal custom in such matters, were given gay uniforms of white trimmed with red. The reason for the choice of these particular colors, if it was more than caprice, is lost to us today. But it must have been a fortunate selection, for the white and red was maintained until years after the Civil War, disappearing at length in that pall of sobriety that enveloped all male clothing toward the end of the nineteenth century.

[Uniform regulations, September 4, 1816; R. Ernest Dupuy, *Where They Have Trod* (New York, 1940); Winfield Scott, *Memoirs* (New York, 1864), I, 128-29; McBarron, *op. cit.*, 196; contemporary prints and paintings in the Academy Library; MS "History of the U. S. M. A. Band and Detachment of Field Musicians" (AGO 997499), in The National Archives.]

Cadet   Bandsman

UNITED STATES MILITARY ACADEMY · 1825

PLATE 9. Common Militia, 1830

THE MILITIA as Americans knew it in the nineteenth century was a characteristically Anglo-Saxon institution. It rested on the democratic ideal that every able bodied man owed his country military service. But it never worked, for its nullifying flaw was the delusion that each such man would and could by his own effort transform himself into a soldier over night. Our forefathers were busy with other matters, and the militia system, in the final analysis, was simply a reflection of their lack of interest in military affairs.

Although Washington declared that he found the militia more hurtful than of service, although no one else, save in empty political oration, has ever uttered or written a serious work in its defense, the system remained a part of our laws until 1903. Actually after 1825 it lingered on only in rural areas, and by 1850 it had died everywhere unmourned. Not a single militia organization served in the Mexican War.

The militiamen shown here may be considered typical of the country at large. Each man has (or should have) his "good musket or firelock, a sufficient bayonet," and all the other paraphernalia required of him by law. The scene is laid at one of the three or four annual drills which were about as effective as the picnics they resembled. No uniforms were provided; the few suggested in the plate represent relics of some former war or service in a Volunteer company. Only the wealthier officers possessed real martial dress.

Yet general muster day was an event of great importance in rural neighborhoods; usually it was held at the county seat. Families drove there from miles around in wagons loaded down with children, food and drink, and produce from the farm. Trading was an important feature of the day. Beside the drill, there were speeches, horse and foot races, wrestling, pole-climbing, and chasing of greased pigs. Real rough-and-tumble fist fights were arranged between such local celebrities as the Woolly Wolf from Blackwater and the Ring-tailed Painter from the Miami bottoms. There was ample food for all, plenty of hard "likker" for the men, and often an old darky selling cider, spruce beer, and ginger cakes for the ladies. At night there was a dance in which all took part. To the scraping fiddles young and old did the pigeon wing, the double shuffle, or the other steps of the period; at length a Virginia reel, with its curtseys and sweeping measures, served as a pleasant ending. It was great fun and undeniably useful, but it certainly wasn't military.

[Emory Upton, *Military Policy of the United States* (Washington, 1907); Rollins Bingham, "An Old Missouri Town," in *Missouri Historical Review*, VIII (1914), 213-15; contemporary prints and newspaper articles.]

COMMON MILITIA · 1830

PLATE 10. 7th Infantry, 1835

Far out along the Arkansas River, on the edge of the Cherokee Country in what is now Oklahoma, lay Fort Gibson. Within its stockade exploring parties bought their last stores before pushing out into the West. Here Indians—Osages, Cherokees, Choctaws, and Creeks—came to trade, make treaties, and see the sights. Up to its landing puffed the squat river steamers, their bars and lounges milling with gamblers, traders, scouts, and all the riff-raff of the frontier. And here, for many years, the soldiers of the 7th Infantry drilled and died of fever and did their part in the policing of the Southwest.

Fort Gibson was founded by the regiment in 1824. Matthew Arbuckle was colonel at the time, and for nearly twenty years he and his organization made this their headquarters. Throughout most of the period the garrison consisted of several companies and the regimental Field and Staff and Band. The latter was the pride of the regiment and the frontier. It was somewhat a "private" affair for, although the musicians were enlisted soldiers, the many additional expenses incident to military music on the Great Plains were borne by the officers and men of the garrison.

The soldier of the 7th is a first sergeant, as is indicated by the epaulettes and sash. His service of over ten years is shown by the chevrons on his sleeve—the forerunner of our modern "hash marks." He wears an undress jacket, which for parade he would exchange for a dark blue tail-coat. His fatigue cap is of cloth, equipped with a "poke" or visor. Were he a private he would wear a waistbelt, a new innovation to keep his equipment from flapping about. Being then new for enlisted men, it was not regulation; each soldier had to buy one out of his meagre pay.

The bass drummer is in a special uniform, designed more than likely by Colonel Arbuckle himself. In 1831 the Adjutant General had allowed regimental commanders this privilege, although it had been a custom long before then. His sky blue coat and black vulture's plumes must have made a brave showing as the band marched and counter-marched before the line of companies drawn up at parade.

[William Brown Morrison, *Military Posts and Camps in Oklahoma* (Oklahoma City, 1936), 28-47; *Army and Navy Chronicle*, April 7, 1836, page 221; uniform regulations, June 11, 1832; A. G. O., General Orders No. 54, September 29, 1831; MSS, Commissary General's Letter Book L, page 140, and Order Book, 1830-36, page 494, in The National Archives; uniforms in the National Museum, Washington, D. C.]

First Sergeant in fatigue uniform　　　　*Bandsman in full dress*

7th **INFANTRY** · 1835

PLATE 11. State Volunteer Corps, 1840

DISTINCT BOTH from the common militia and the regular forces stood the colorful companies and battalions of chartered State Volunteers. Nominally part of the militia, they were in fact independent, almost private organizations. Not a few dated back to the eighteenth century; all were proud, willful, and somewhat theatrical. Since membership in the Volunteers involved no little expenditure of time and money, the companies were jealous of the prerogatives allowed by their charters.

By the 1840's these Volunteers were a recognized part of the life of all of the Eastern cities, closely akin to the fire companies and target clubs which flourished throughout that era. Each had its club rooms, its trophies, and its colors. Names, uniforms, and officers were chosen by popular vote, and the companies reflected most of the races which then made up our population. Hibernia Greens and German Guards were as familiar as the native American corps. The companies were available for call in local emergencies and many a unit rendered valuable service during riots and catastrophes.

In street parades, of course, they showed up at their finest. First in the procession marched a detail of sappers with rented beards and broad-axes, next came a brass band with the drum major in a towering bearskin, and behind that rode the staff on gayly bedecked horses. Each company as it passed was accompanied by its "honorary members" who paraded but did not drill regularly, its Negro servants bearing buckets of water or stronger fare, and at times its silverware and trophies suspended from poles.

The corps shown here are examples of the better class of Volunteer. On the right is an officer of the Light Guard, one of the more fashionable companies of New York City. Until 1831 its uniform had been blue, and the change in that year to the red jacket and high busby—more than suggestive of the British Grenadier Guards—did not rest too well with the Irish elements of that city. Yet the uniform was maintained until 1844 when a white jacket was adopted. In time the Light Guard became the Old Guard, now a veteran's society, and the white coat, blue trousers, and bearskin hat is still worn by that body. Marches, songs, and even a variety of champagne punch were named for the Light Guard, but when the Civil War broke its members became the officers who drilled and led many a Union regiment.

The other Volunteer comes from Boston. He is a color-bearer of the New England Guards, an equally celebrated corps. His blue uniform, tall shako with the heavy brass plate, and flowing cock's feathers are more typical in color and design of the Volunteer dress of the period than any other style. The standard he carries bears the arms of the State of Massachusetts and was undoubtedly presented to the unit with much ceremony and oration by the patriotic ladies of Boston.

[*U. S. Military Magazine,* 1839-1842; Frederick P. Todd, "Our National Guard," in *Military Affairs,* Summer, 1941 (V, 73-86); contemporary music covers and descriptions.]

Color-bearer, New England Guards   *Officer, New York Light Guard*

STATE VOLUNTEER CORPS · 1840

PLATE 12. Texas Rangers and Mississippi Rifles, 1846

THE ARMY which pushed southwest from the Rio Grande into Mexico under General Taylor was a motley crew. The divisions toiling along the road to Monterey, through the dust and thorns and the baking heat that made every mile a misery, included both Regulars and volunteers. There were infantry in sky blue, clanking field batteries in blue and red, Western units in homespun kits, and many others in no uniform at all. Among these last was a company of striking appearance; its men rode ahead of the entire column, scattered out in front of the pioneers and screening the advance. They were McCulloch's Texas Rangers—the finest scouts in the army.

The Texans rode casually on quick, tough horses, but their eyes never ceased to rove under wide hat-brims for the spot of color or the flash of sun on a lance tip that signalled a Mexican patrol. Their clothing was of the roughest sort. For an upper garment a coarse red or blue shirt or a greasy fringed hunting jacket sufficed; their trousers were tucked into "mule's ear" boots or "breed" leggins. Most wore the low crowned slouch hat so familiar in the Southwest of that day.

Each ranger carried a heavy flintlock rifle, powderhorn, and bullet pouch, a large bowie knife, and sometimes one of the new Colt revolvers. From his saddle hung a braided lariat to be used as a tether, a bag of parched and pounded corn, a canteen, and blanket or *serape*. Many had acquired Mexican equipment—high-pommelled saddles of beautifully tooled leather, silver studded bridles, and the long, sharp spurs of a *vacquero*.

In the same column marched a unit of very different sort. They too were riflemen, but they carried the new percussion weapon just being issued to the Regulars. Their clothing was equally simple—red flannel shirts, Panama hats, and white duck trousers, but the men were not frontiersmen. At their head rode Colonel Jefferson Davis, a West Pointer, and behind each company marched Negro servants. For this volunteer regiment, the Mississippi Rifles, was composed in the main of sons of wealthy Southern planters who could afford the luxuries of trained leadership and personal servants.

Yet there was nothing pampered about the Rifles; few outfits in Taylor's force marched or fought harder. They brought back from Mexico a record worthy of the toughest veterans and were cited by the general for "highly conspicuous gallantry and steadiness." The weapon they carried was the model 1841 percussion rifle, manufactured by the government. Colonel Davis had demanded that his regiment be furnished with these instead of flintlocks, and they were put to good use; the model has been known ever since as the "Mississippi." No bayonets were furnished, however, and the men had to be ready to use their long bowie knives when the Mexican cavalry galloped up too close for comfort.

[Justin H. Smith, *The War with Mexico* (New York, 1919), I, 225 *ff.*; Robert McElroy, *Jefferson Davis* . . . (New York, 1937), I, 74-94; S. C. Smith, *Chile con Carne* (New York, 1857), page 94; contemporary sketches.]

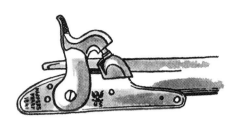

TEXAS RANGERS AND MISSISSIPPI RIFLES · 1846

PLATE 13. 3rd Artillery, 1847

"A LITTLE MORE grape, Captain Bragg!"

These may not have been the exact words, but this celebrated message, sent by General Taylor in the final and critical stage of the Battle of Buena Vista, has become a permanent part of American military tradition. Of the episode Taylor later wrote: "Captain Bragg, who had just arrived from the left, was ordered at once into battery. Without infantry to support him and at imminent risk of losing his guns, he came rapidly into action, the Mexican line being but a few yards from the muzzle of his pieces. The first discharge of cannister caused the enemy to hesitate, the second and third drove him back in disorder and saved the day."

Captain Braxton Bragg commanded Company C, 3d Artillery. It was the only fully-mounted "horse artillery" in the entire army. Each of its six guns and six caissons were pulled by six-horse teams. Each gun was served by twelve men, individually mounted; no cannoneers rode on the boxes. The men of this company were authorized a distinctive uniform—alone of all the Artillery, they wore dark blue jackets like the Dragoons, but trimmed with red instead of yellow lace. In efficiency, discipline and drill the Company led all the outfits in Taylor's army.

In the four Regular Artillery regiments at the outbreak of the Mexican War, there were only four companies (one to each regiment) equipped with field guns. After the war began, an additional "light" company was authorized for each regiment, and three were equipped in time to see service during the war. The remaining forty companies of Regular Artillery were stationed in peacetime in the forts along the Atlantic coast, there to handle the heavy guns. In the Mexican War, most of these "foot" companies served in the field as infantry. Now and again one would be given an artillery mission with siege pieces or with captured field guns and makeshift teams, and the artilleryman of those days had to be versed in weapons of all calibers.

It would be untrue to say that the cannoneers enjoyed their service as infantrymen, but they performed it gallantly nonetheless. The 3d Artillery was no exception. Time and again the value of their training as cannoneers was proven. Among the first to storm into the *tête-de-pont* at Churubusco was a handful of the Regiment. Seizing a Mexican 8-pounder, the men turned it on the enemy and effectively broke up further resistance. These foot artillerymen of the Third were uniformed and equipped as infantry when so serving, but they never gave up their yellow lace and brass buttons. These things, after all, had distinguished them from foot soldiers since 1776 and, to the cannoneer, such distinction was important.

[William E. Birkhimer, *Historical Sketch of . . . the Artillery, United States Army* (Washington, 1884); *Ordnance Manual*, 1841; uniform regulations, 1849; MSS in QMG papers, The National Archives.]

Foot Artilleryman, fatigue uniform   Driver and team, Light Company C, fatigue uniform

3rd ARTILLERY · 1847

PLATE 14. Corps of Engineers and the Mexican Spy Company, 1847

THE OFFICERS of the Corps of Engineers and the affiliated topographical service were the elite of the Army, chosen from those graduates of the Military Academy having the highest stand. The work performed by the Corps in times of peace was varied and exacting. Its officers explored, mapped, and projected the long wagon routes across the continent; they developed the inland waterways throughout the Great Lakes and the valleys of the Ohio and Mississippi; they planned the railroads which spanned the West; they labored to control floods and deepen harbors; and they constructed the masonry forts which today line our eastern coast from Maine to Florida.

The record of the Corps in war was no less distinguished. Many generals of the line commenced their careers as engineers. It was their duty on campaign to construct temporary fortifications, bridges, and roads and to destroy enemy obstacles. They also planned marches and positions, estimated needs in men and supplies, and in general assisted in the intricate job of managing an army. Above all, they had to secure intelligence about the enemy, reconnoiter his positions, and plan the best ways of driving him out. In short, the Engineer officer of the nineteenth century performed almost all the functions which today are assigned to a general staff; in particular, he was the intelligence officer.

Intelligence work of this type is dependent upon the receipt of accurate and prompt information concerning the enemy's dispositions and movements. To obtain such information special scout or spy detachments were formed, usually composed of natives of the region being fought over. Many of our boyhood heroes, such as Davy Crockett and "Buffalo Bill" Cody, made their early reputations in this dangerous work. In the Vera Cruz campaign of 1847 such scouting was performed by a unit called the Spy Company under command of Manuel Domínguez. Men of different nationalities served in its ranks, but for the most part it comprised former highwaymen, like Domínguez himself, familiar with every inch of the roads between Vera Cruz and Mexico.

The Spy Company rendered faithful and efficient service. It screened the advance of the American force and searched out enemy positions, and detachments even entered the Mexican capital in disguise. The men were armed in their native fashion with lance, carbine, and sabre, supplied in part by Scott's quartermasters. At first they appear to have worn grey uniforms similar in cut to the American, but later a green cavalry jacket, trimmed with red, became the regular dress. Their low crowned Mexican hats of black felt were trimmed with a wide red band. These, like the trousers and most of the other articles of apparel, were of local origin. The gay dress of the scout contrasts sharply with the fatigue uniform of the engineer. Its trimmings of black velvet and generally somber tone, however, were quite in keeping with the dignity of the Corps.

[Otto Zirckel, *Tagebuch geschrieben waehrend der nordamerikischen—mexikanischen Campagne* . . . (Halle, 1849), pages 116-17; Smith, *op. cit.*, II, 362; uniform regulations, 1841; material in the Museo Nacional, Mexico.]

Sergeant of Spies

Lieutenant of Engineers in frock coat

CORPS OF ENGINEERS AND THE MEXICAN SPY COMPANY · 1847

PLATE 15. 1st Dragoons, 1851

As THE military frontier drew further westward into the plains country, the Army met a new kind of antagonist in the mounted Indian. Cavalry had been abolished in 1815 as a measure of economy, and the slow moving infantry found themselves hard put to protect the great caravan routes pushing out into New Mexico, California, and Oregon.

A more agile force was urgently needed. In 1832 a Battalion of Mounted Rangers had been established, and in the next year it was expanded into a regiment of Dragoons. Escort and reconnaissance duty commenced even before organization was completed, and one of the regiment's first missions was a five hundred mile march into the upper Red River under General Leavenworth. George Catlin, the celebrated painter of Western scenes, accompanied the expedition, writing as he was about to depart, "I start this morning with the dragoons for the Pawnee country, but God only knows where that is."

The hard frontier service and the wars in Florida and Mexico which followed left no room in the Dragoons for other than tough, courageous troopers, nor much opportunity for full dress parades. There still were occasions, of course, when the men could wear plumed shakos and long tailed coats and trot by in review to the music of the regimental band, but much of the time they more closely resembled banditti than soldiers. The Dragoons, alone in all the Army, were permitted to wear mustachios—a distinction in which they took great pride. With long flowing hair, rings in their ears, and a brace of pistols in their belts, they rode through the Indian country enforcing the White Man's law.

It was thus that a newspaper artist named White saw and sketched them at Fort Snelling in 1851. To impress the Indian chiefs gathered at the Fort for conference, they had brought their full dress uniforms. In the accompanying sketch there is the trooper just back from a scout, his Hall carbine slung handily from the saddle. Over his legs he wears "breed" leggins to protect them from the high brush, and the handkerchief is ready to be pulled over his face to keep out the dust clouds of a cavalry column.

The chief trumpeter in the plate is wearing what was to be the last of the red uniforms which had distinguished Army musicians from other soldiers and which the Marine Corps Band continues to wear today for full dress. The trumpeter's tailed coat was already out of fashion, however, for in this very year the dress regulations had ordered all of the Army into the frock coat then worn by the armies of Europe. "Tails" had gone the way of armor and the cocked hat.

[Albert G. Brackett, *History of the U. S. Cavalry* . . . (New York, 1865); Percival G. Lowe, *Five Years a Dragoon* (Kansas City, 1906); uniform regulations, May 1, 1847; uniforms in the National Museum, Washington, D. C.; MS "Collection of sketches made during the Sioux troubles of 1851," in the New York Public Library.]

Corporal in campaign uniform   *Chief trumpeter in full dress*

FIRST DRAGOONS · 1851

PLATE 16. 7th Regiment, New York State Militia, 1861

O<small>N THE</small> morning of April 12, 1861, that grim morning ushered in by the long echoes of gun-fire over Charleston Harbor, the people of the North awoke to find themselves at war and their capital unguarded and in grave danger. The forces of the Confederacy were gathering in Virginia, and the small Regular Army lay scattered in a hundred tiny posts from Key West to Puget Sound. As usual, we were not ready. The only troops to whom President Lincoln could turn for aid in this emergency were the long neglected Volunteer militias of the Northern States. On these he called for 75,000 men to be sent at once and to serve for the period of three months.

To this call the loyal States replied as quickly and ably as they could. Those that had possessed enough foresight to keep up their Volunteer corps—their old independent companies of uniformed militia—were able to act at once. The call went out on April 15, and four days later a small Pennsylvania force had arrived in Washington and a Massachusetts regiment (the 6th Militia) was fighting its way through Baltimore. Each succeeding day found other troops on the road until, as the *New York Tribune* estimated, in less than two weeks 35,000 men were in the Capital or en route there, and 20,000 were ready for transportation. General Scott was then able to write that the city was safe.

Among the first to go was the 7th New York, already a famous unit with fifty-five years of history and the adjective "silk stocking" to its credit. Although its rolls did include many an old New York name, the 7th was no more than typical of regiments which existed in all the large cities and had grown out of the former independent companies. In both the North and South these were the units which responded to the first call, which served as models and drillmasters for the huge civilian armies which had to be raised, and from the ranks of which came so many of the new leaders. The 7th alone furnished over five hundred officers to the Union Army.

In its splendid New York armory there hangs a painting by Thomas Nast (he who later fought the Tweed Ring) of the regiment's departure on that April day in 1861. In the museum nearby one can see photographs of some of the men who went with it, posed in full marching gear. From these sources, and from other objects in the museum, the details of this drawing are taken. The grey uniform, the low kepi so familiar at this period, the heavy knapsack and blanket, and the wide white belts all bespeak the crack militia regiment of the time. However, the up-to-date rifle with Maynard primer, the sturdy overcoat, and the ample equipment indicate a state of accoutrement far ahead of most units of the early Civil War.

[A. Howard Meneely, *The War Department, 1861* (New York, 1928); Emmons Clark, *History of the Seventh Regiment of New York* (New York, 1890); regimental orders, photographs, and other items in the regimental museum.]

Private in overcoat

Private in full field equipment

7th REGIMENT · NEW YORK STATE MILITIA · 1861

PLATE 17. Louisiana Zouaves, 1861

In the days of the Civil War the company of from fifty to one hundred men was the basic military unit. In 1861 every city, town, and village throughout the land provided one or more—raised usually by some prominent man—to the armies of either the North or the South. Enthusiasm and confidence is reflected in the names they chose: Coldwater Cadets, Genesee Rangers, or Irwin Invincibles. Usually without uniforms and arms—and certainly without training and discipline—they poured into the state camps and into the regiments then being formed. Their independent glory was short; their brave titles were soon lost in the anonymity of the larger units. Thus, for example, was the Tyranny Unmasked Artillery transformed into Company K, 47th Virginia.

One is immediately struck by the great number of Zouave units among these early volunteers. This widespread craze was not due to any particular affinity with France, but really originated in the meeting of a penniless law clerk named Elmer E. Ellsworth and a French sword master in Chicago. To Ellsworth the Frenchman, who had served in the Zouaves during the Crimean War, described the rapid drill of the famous Algerian corps. Together they worked out a modified manual and introduced the movements and the novel dress to a company Ellsworth had formed in Chicago. He demanded rigid training and constant practice, and as a result his Zouaves drilled flawlessly. In 1860 he took the company on an epoch making trip throughout the East, even to West Point, and everywhere it was greeted with wild enthusiasm. It was a critical moment in our national history and the idea caught the fancy and was copied by hundreds of the companies then forming. So was the American Zouave born.

An excellent example of such corps was the 1st Battalion, Louisiana Zouaves. It was formed during March and April 1861 in New Orleans and mustered into Confederate service for the war. Its ranks contained many men of French descent and its commands were at first given in that language, but a glance at its rolls shows an even larger number of German, Irish, and English names like many another regiment on both sides. It had a splendid record and saw the hardest kind of fighting from the beginning to the end of the conflict.

The uniform of both officers and men were almost an exact copy of the French original: short Algerian jacket, red fez or kepi, baggy trousers, and broad sash. Their belt plates carried the device of Louisiana, a pelican feeding its young. In this kit they left New Orleans in April, but so poorly were these early uniforms made that in June most of the companies reported their clothing "used up." By July, after the fight at Bull Run, they were "destitute."

[*Annual Report of the Adjutant General of Louisiana, 1893*, 27; Charles A. Ingraham, "Colonel Elmer E. Ellsworth," in *Wisconsin Magazine of History*, I, 349-74; battalion rolls and papers in The National Archives; contemporary photographs and descriptions.]

Captain and Zouave

LOUISIANA ZOUAVES · 1861

PLATE 18. Federal Infantry, 1862

In the American Civil War, as in every war for centuries past, the dominant role was played by the Infantry—the "Queen of Battles." In numbers alone the record is impressive; over 1,700 regiments saw service as combat infantry in the Union Army.

Although the regiment remained the permanent unit of organization, for tactical purposes several were combined to form a brigade. Before long some brigades took on a personality of their own as fighting outfits and became more famous than the regiments they contained. Two such, the Vermont and Iron Brigades, are illustrated here.

The Vermont Brigade was unusual in the Union Army in being composed entirely of regiments from one State. What is more, it marched in the Grand Review of 1865 with the same five regiments with which it was organized at the beginning of the war. The Brigade suffered the greatest loss of life of any similar unit in the Union Army. At the Wilderness it lost 1,269 men and officers—killed, wounded and missing; within a week it had lost 1,645 more, out of its remaining strength of 2,800. Despite these staggering casualties the Brigade maintained throughout its reputation for gallantry and dash.

Equally rugged was the Iron Brigade of the West, which took the heaviest losses in proportion to its strength of any Union brigade of the war. Its fighting record was established at Antietam and renewed at Second Manassas, Gettysburg, South Mountain, The Wilderness, Spotsylvania, and on a dozen other fields. For much of its life it was made up of the 2d, 6th and 7th Wisconsin, the 19th Indiana, and the 24th Michigan.

The Westerners of the Iron Brigade preferred black, brimmed hats to the regulation blue caps. When he learned this their commander, General John Gibbon, had black felt hats issued to his entire brigade. Quickly the Confederates came to recognize these tough black-hatted adversaries and gave the outfit a new name: the Black Hat Brigade.

In the field the Union soldier was allowed much freedom in the matter of clothes, and black hats, battered into a hundred shapes, were not, of course, confined to soldiers of the Iron Brigade. They were worn on campaign by many Union regiments, the Western outfits in particular. Indeed, they came to distinguish the veteran soldier, and the Confederate skirmishers moved with far greater caution when they noticed black hats on the opposing line of battle.

Both of these soldiers wear the insignia of their respective brigades. The use of these patches originated in June 1862, when General Philip Kearney ordered a piece of scarlet cloth worn by all men of his 3d Division, 3d Corps. The idea quickly caught on and by the middle of 1863 most of the elements of the Army of the Potomac had adopted some sort of device. The basic design was that of the corps, while its color usually represented a specific division within the corps. The "sphere" of the 1st Corps and the "Greek cross" of the 6th were well known and respected symbols on all the Eastern battlefields.

[William Fox, *Regimental Losses in the American Civil War* (Albany, N.Y., 1889); John Gibbon, *Personal Recollections* (N.Y., 1928); *Military Collector & Historian*, IV, 35-38; contemporary photographs and descriptions.]

Iron Brigade of the West   *Vermont Brigade*

FEDERAL INFANTRY · 1862

PLATE 19. Stuart's Cavalry Division, C.S.A., 1862

THE EXPERIENCE gained in cavalry operations against the restless Indians of the Plains stood the South in good stead in 1861. Comparatively few men in the North knew anything about riding or the care of horses. Its cavalry had to be built from the bottom up, and it takes a long time to make a cavalryman.

Not so with the Confederacy. Its men of all walks of life and ages took naturally to exercises in which the horse and rifle played a prominent part. To train such men to become able cavalry soldiers was a comparatively easy task; indeed, many of the Southern militia companies were already mounted. It took the Union Army two years to catch up with the Confederates in this field, but from then on, under leaders like Sheridan, Wilson, and Buford—and with an ever improving supply of horses, weapons, and equipment—the Federal cavalry forged ahead and played a leading part in the final outcome of the War.

Few careers in our military past equal in romance that of J. E. B. Stuart, commander of the cavalry of Lee's Army of Northern Virginia. He has justly been called the most brilliant light cavalry leader of his time. He was gay, daring, resourceful, and picturesque, and these qualities were handed on to the men under him. Starting with barely three hundred sabres, he built his force into a splendid command that rarely failed to outwit the slower Federal horse. His regiments came from several states, but principally from Virginia. With the Division travelled the swift guns of the Stuart Horse Artillery, commanded at first by John Pelham, called "the gallant." Every man of his was mounted and every field piece tacked for the tough job of keeping up with the cavalry.

Stuart's qualities were reflected in his dress and in that of his officers. Most of them discarded the long regulation coat while in the field for the much freer mounted jacket, the lining of which, when buttoned back, made a gay flash of color. Following their leader's example, many of the officers wore an ostrich plume in their wide brimmed hats. Once Stuart's hat was captured. "I intend," he wrote, "to make the Yankees pay for that hat," and in less than a week he had seized the personal baggage of the Union general responsible.

Great high boots, sash, a long revolver, and the heavy sabre of the period completed the costume. Light blue was the regulation color for the trousers, but corduroy, washed almost white, was favored by the *beau sabreur* of North and South alike. The artillery major, more conservative, has the regulation kepi. Two years later this article, together with much of the other fine clothing, had disappeared, and the Confederate officer and private alike were happy to wear anything that would keep them warm.

[*Regulations for the Army of the Confederate States, 1862*, article 47; John W. Thomason, *Jeb Stuart* (New York, 1934); uniforms and photographs in the Confederate Museum, Richmond, Virginia.]

Colonel of Cavalry   *Major of Horse Artillery*

STUART'S CAVALRY DIVISION, C. S. A. · 1862

PLATE 20. Confederate Infantry, 1863

Out of the scattered and incomplete records of the Confederate Infantry come accounts of heroism and endurance which easily rival those from the North. The Confederate armies lost, in the aggregate, nearly 10 percent in killed and mortally wounded, while the same loss among Northern troops was 5 percent. Most of this was in the Infantry. Although this is not a fair comparison of valor, for there were over 300 Northern regiments which never saw battle, it gives an idea of sacrifices made on the Confederate side.

At Antietam the 1st Texas suffered 82 percent casualties without flinching. In the next two years we have record of at least forty-two Confederate regiments which lost in one day's fighting over half their strength and still remained in the line. There are many vivid descriptions of Garnett's Virginia Brigade, of Pickett's Division, in its celebrated charge at Gettysburg. But what the charge meant in human endurance comes out of statistics; Garnett's Brigade entered the fight with 1,427 men and returned to Seminary Ridge with only 486 on their feet.

When the Confederate infantryman took the field in 1861 he carried everything he, the government and his family could supply, often including a revolver, a bowie knife, and a long list of non-military possessions ranging from banjos to bibles. The first march usually saw the end of the heaviest and least essential objects, and from then on the soldier continued to reduce his load. His knapsack was the first thing to go; a few personal items rolled inside a blanket and slung over one shoulder sufficed. Canteens were useful but in time even they were thrown away in favor of a tin cup. The heavy coat was replaced by a short jacket and the tall boots by tough broghans. So the Confederate trimmed down until, by 1863, he was the lightest equipped soldier in the world.

The grey jacket was almost universally worn save in warm weather when a cotton shirt sufficed. Cotton could be more easily washed than flannel or merino, and vermin did not seem to propagate in it so easily. The comfort an overcoat gave in cold weather was never worth the trouble of carrying it around the rest of the year, and the soldier who slept out of doors soon learned to do without it. Many men continued to wear grey caps, but slouch hats were more popular. For trousers almost anything served, although sky-blue kersey (often captured from Union stocks) or cotton ones stained with butternut were the more common kinds.

The Confederate foot soldier sometimes dispensed with his percussion cap and cartridge boxes and carried his caps and cartridges in his pockets, and even bayonets were thrown aside if officers were not watchful. A haversack, a blanket, a rubber blanket, a rifle musket and a handful of ammunition, a cup or pannikin, and the absolute essentials of clothing constituted the minimum for the Rebel infantry. Their devotion and powers of endurance overcame the hardships incurred with such a kit and made them easily the equal of their well-equipped opponents.

[Carlton McCarthy, *Detailed Minutiae of Soldier Life in the Army of Northern Virginia, 1861-1865* (Richmond, 1882); Fox, *Regimental Losses*, op. cit., 552-71.]

CONFEDERATE INFANTRY · 1863

PLATE 21. New York Zouaves, 1863

The state of New York put more zouave regiments into the Civil War, it would seem, than all the other States on both sides of the conflict combined. Why this was true is difficult to say unless the abnormally large number of foreign-born in New York City took more readily to colorful uniforms and rapid drill. Actually, these zouave outfits contained a substantial percentage of native-born soldiers and were not, in the aggregate, noted for containing any one particular nationality.

New York zouave regiments ranged in quality from very superior to very bad. The Civil War historian William F. Fox has included several among his "Three Hundred Fighting Regiments" of the Union Army, and the two selected for this picture are among that gallant company.

The first regiment will be known to every student of the Civil War, for it was truly one of the great units—Duryee's Zouaves, the 5th New York. During its entire active service it served in a division of Regulars and fully maintained its right to be there. General Sykes called it the best volunteer organization he had ever seen; it was noted throughout the Army of the Potomac for its gay uniform, but even more for its precision of drill and steadiness under fire. At the Battle of Gaines' Mill, under Hiram Duryee, it faced a hail of Confederate musketry which cut down one-third of its men. After an especially deadly volley it halted in line to count off anew so that its movements would not be deranged by the gaps in its ranks.

The Duryee Zouaves wore a uniform not too different from its French prototype: blue jacket and vest, blue sash, baggy red trousers and a red fez. On parade the men added a white havelock or turban around the fez, and all wore long white gaiters. Their first clothing was manufactured in New York City by private contract, but thereafter the regiment received its distinctive dress through the Federal quartermasters.

The 44th New York carried the rather theatrical name of Ellsworth's Avengers. It was raised principally in upstate New York, although its men came from every county in the State. Only unmarried, able-bodied volunteers under thirty years of age, standing at least five feet eight inches, were accepted. Each volunteer had to prove he was of good moral character. Because of these unusual requirements, the Regiment's enlisted personnel was the finest of any in the service, averaging 22 years in age and over 5 feet 10 inches in height.

For the first year or so of its service the 44th New York wore on all occasions the modified style of zouave dress illustrated; thereafter this uniform was reserved for dress parades and the regulation Army fatigue blouse was worn in the field. From first to last the outfit earned a high reputation for valor, perhaps its best known exploit being the part it played in the seizure and defense of Little Round Top during the second day at Gettysburg.

[Alfred Davenport, *Camp and Field Life of the Fifth New York Infantry* (New York, 1879); Eugene A. Nash, *A History of the Forty-Fourth Regiment New York Volunteer Infantry* ... (Chicago, 1911); Fox, *Regimental Losses, op. cit.*, 191, 195; contemporary photographs.]

5th New York   44th New York

NEW YORK ZOUAVES · 1863

PLATE 22. Corps D'Afrique, 1864

Negro freedmen fought in all of our earlier wars. It was a colored man who shot the British Major Pitcairn from the earth-works on Bunker Hill. Two of General Jackson's best battalions in the Battle of New Orleans were the Free Men of Color under Fortier and D'Aquin. It was thus inevitable that the question of recruiting Negroes for more than manual labor, that is for actual combat service, should arise early in the Civil War.

On the Northern side, after considerable hesitation and trial, a start was made in the fall of 1862 with units raised in the occupied areas of South Carolina and Louisiana. The practice later became general and embraced both free Negroes and emancipated slaves. Naming these new regiments presented something of a problem, for it was deemed wise to distinguish them from other units. The Federal authorities at New Orleans worried over this awhile, then hit upon the expedient of borrowing a title from abroad. They called their colored division the Corps d'Afrique. The name lasted until the spring of 1864 when the Corps was amalgamated with all other Negro units into a component bearing the more forthright title of U. S. Colored Troops.

The Corps d'Afrique had one regiment of heavy artillery whose duty it was to man the fortress cannon in the Defences of New Orleans. This is did for five years, although it was never called upon to fire the giant Parrotts and Columbiads at an enemy force. Heavy artillery were primarily fortress troops, and their more stationary jobs gave them ample opportunity for parades and reviews. This was particularly true with the big, gorgeous regiments in the Defences of Washington. Their comparative comfort and security—which they were careful to advertise—made them a popular branch until Grant, in 1864, ordered them to the front as infantry—to the glee of the rest of the army.

The heavy artilleryman wears the long coat, plumed felt hat, and brass shoulder scales of the Civil War full dress uniform. His sword was a peculiar type worn by non-commissioned officers of this branch of the service. His companion wears a modified form of this same uniform with the "frogging" of a musician and the "bummer's cap" so common throughout the Northern army.

The latter soldier is a member of one of the brigade bands which had replaced the regimental bands in 1862. The Corps d'Afrique had two such units, composed of colored musicians recruited in the North. Although men might argue in those days over the merit of the Negro as a combat soldier, none could dispute his preeminence in the field of military music. For generations he had served in this capacity, but now he was even more in his element with the brass bands that had come into use. Marches and parades were not the only duties of the Corps bands, however; there were concerts to be given and dances for the white officers, for service was not very strenuous in the sleepy Mississippi garrisons of the Union Army.

[*The Photographic History of the Civil War* (New York, 1911), V, 13-154; G. W. Williams, *History of Negro Troops in War of Rebellion* (New York, 1888); uniform regulations of March 13, 1861, modified December 16, 1861; clothing returns in The National Archives.]

Brigade Bandsman   *Sergeant of Heavy Artillery*

CORPS D'AFRIQUE · 1864

PLATE 23. 7th Cavalry, 1876

FOLLOWING the Civil War the Army returned to its old job of guarding the frontier. In this the cavalry, now expanded to ten regiments, played the leading role. For almost fifteen years the desultory warfare continued, the troops now fighting Indians, now protecting them from the more predatory Whites. At last, with the extinction of the buffalo, the long struggle ended, but not before the Indian had gotten in several hard blows at the soldiery.

The cavalry of this period used for their full dress the helmet which had, the world over, generally replaced the shako as the formal military headdress. This distinctive form of hat had its origin in Denmark about 1850. It was adopted by the Prussian army, whose successes in the 1860's and '70's led to its general popularity. England, Russia, the United States, and a host of smaller nations were soon wearing either the spiked helmet or its plumed counterpart. By 1876 they had been issued only to mounted troops in this country, but within a few years all the Army had them.

The field uniform was much simpler. A black felt slouch hat, plain blue coat, and high leather boots made an efficient dress for fighting on the Plains. The cavalryman was armed with the long sabre of the Civil War type, a six-shot revolver, and a carbine. The models of these last two weapons varied considerably, as did the other parts of equipment, for this was an era of great experimentation with ordnance.

It was in this field uniform that the 7th Cavalry participated in its best known and most tragic campaign, that against the hostile Sioux which led to the Battle of the Little Big Horn. Here Lieutenant Colonel Custer and five troops of the regiment were surrounded by an overwhelming force of Indians and killed to a man. In the battle proper the soldiers did not wear their sabres—these had been left behind with the regimental train—but fought only with the single-shot carbines and the revolvers that made up the rest of their armament. It is worthwhile to note that many of the Sioux were armed with repeating Winchester rifles of a far greater range and faster rate of fire than the Springfields carried by the cavalrymen.

[War Department, General Orders No. 92, October 26, 1872, and subsequent amendments; Ordnance Department, *Ordnance Memoranda No. 18* (1873); Charles Francis Bates, *Custer's Indian Battles* (Bronxville, N.Y., 1936); contemporary photographs.]

Trooper, field service

Corporal, full dress

7th CAVALRY · 1876

PLATE 24. Organized Militia, 1885

THE STORY OF our State Volunteer Militia of the nineteenth century is one of steady incorporation of the independently chartered companies into regiments, of increasing uniformity and improvement in training, and of gradual Federalization. Instead of Volunteers they came to be called the Organized Militia, and from that the name was changed in 1903 to the National Guard. In each State the process varied, but the overall trend was unmistakable.

In an earlier plate we saw men of two chartered companies of the 1840's. Further along are shown soldiers of an organized regiment of State Militia in 1861 as it marched off to the Civil War. Here we see militiamen of a quarter century later. The men are from two old and celebrated outfits, the First Troop Philadelphia City Cavalry and the Richmond Light Infantry Blues. In a way, both of the units are exceptions to our first statement, for the City Troop in 1885 was still an independent chartered company and it remains so today. The Blues had by 1885 twice been incorporated into the 1st Regiment, Virginia Volunteers, and twice made independent again. But in 1894 the Blues were expanded into a battalion and finally, in 1920, they returned to the First Virginia (now the 176th Infantry) as the senior battalion.

When, on Christmas Day in 1776, Washington crossed the Delaware in his desperate bid for success at Trenton, he was guarded by a small troop of light horse. He had known the men before, for they had escorted him part way to Boston at the beginning of the war. He knew them as gentlemen riders, volunteers from Philadelphia, and he selected them to be his personal escort. His confidence was not misplaced, for all through that bitter winter campaign they served faithfully, returning to their homes only after the Continental Army had entered winter quarters in comparative safety at Morristown. This troop was the Philadelphia City Cavalry, born in 1774 and still active. It no longer rides horses on campaign, but it still performs the mission of cavalry as the 28th Reconnaissance Company of Pennsylvania's Keystone Division.

The Richmond Blues were formed in 1789 and almost from the beginning the corps wore a blue and white uniform trimmed with silver. These were the colors and metal which distinguished the American Infantryman for so many years. The Blues still maintain this old uniform, one of the few remaining National Guard outfits to have a full dress.

In the War of 1812, in the Army of Northern Virginia from Roanoke Island to Appomatox, in the Army of Cuban Occupation, and as the demonstration regiment at the Infantry School, the Blues—true to their colors—served on foot as dogfaces. Strange to find, then, on leafing through their history, that from 1916 to 1919 they climbed aboard horses. But in that period almost anything could happen, and did, to the National Guard.

[*Army Lineage Book*, II, Infantry; John A. Cutchins, *A Famous Command, the Richmond Light Infantry Blues* (Richmond, 1934); *History of the First Troop Philadelphia City Cavalry, 1774-1874* (Philadelphia, 1875).]

First Troop Philadelphia City Cavalry   *Richmond Light Infantry Blues*

ORGANIZED MILITIA · 1885

PLATE 25. Cuban Expedition, 1898

WITH THE disappearance of our Indian frontier many Americans were ready to believe that the usefulness of the Army had come to an end. But in the late 1890's the conditions in Cuba became intolerable, and the proximity of this island led us gradually into a conflict with Spain. Of course, we were not ready to send an expeditionary force even the two hundred miles to Cuba, but that condition has never given us pause for long. As rapidly as possible a force of Regulars, Organized Militia, and raw volunteers was gathered at Tampa, Florida, which was the port from which we planned to launch the invasion. The types in the plate are characteristic—in looks at least—of the men who made up that body.

The mounted man is a trooper of the 1st U. S. Volunteer Cavalry, familiarly known as the Rough Riders. It was the last of what may be called the "personal regiments," that is, elite units raised and officered by a prominent civilian for a particular war. It had been organized by Theodore Roosevelt, then Assistant Secretary of the Navy, and so popular was he that the ranks of the regiment were filled in less than three weeks. Wisely he asked to serve as second-in-command under Colonel Leonard Wood, a competent Regular, albeit a medical officer. The men who joined were equally as unusual as the commanders. There were cowpunchers, actors, doctors, frontier sheriffs, society leaders, professional gamblers, and college athletes. Every one of them, however, knew how to ride and shoot.

The regiment was armed with the magazine carbine and Western "six-shooter." It received regular mounted equipment, but in the rush to get to the scene of action there was no time to procure uniforms. As a result the Rough Riders at first wore the canvas stable dress of the cavalry—a suitable dress for the tropics but not one which added much to the appearance of the unit.

The man on foot is from the 71st New York Volunteers, one of the old Volunteer militia organizations of New York City. The Merriam Pack on his back was a knapsack of recent invention and questionable value. A complicated system of straps and rods was scientifically designed to distribute the load evenly, but it rarely worked. As a result, many of the packs remained by the Cuban roadside, the men preferring to wrap their belongings into the characteristically American blanket roll. The New Yorker's blue uniform was of the general type worn by the rest of the Expedition. His rifle, a single-shot Springfield, marks him as a militiaman, however, for by then the Regulars had been issued the Krag-Jorgensen magazine weapon.

These were the troops, then, who camped at Tampa in June, 1898, preparing for the invasion of Cuba. The confusion which reigned there is almost unbelievable. Both of the regiments, it is said, had to hold up trains at the point of a pistol in order to obtain transportation to the docks. When they finally did sail all of the horses of the Rough Riders had been left behind.

[J. T. Dickman, ed., *The Santiago Campaign* (Richmond, 1927), pages 102-109, 127-146; Walter Millis, *The Martial Spirit* (Boston, 1937); War Department, General Orders No. 67, June 10, 1898; AGO New York, General Orders No. 11, 1894; contemporary photographs.]

Trooper, Rough Rider, in stable dress   *Private, 71st New York, in full field equipment*

CUBAN EXPEDITION · 1898

PLATE 26. Philippine Scouts, 1904

WHEN THE NEWS arrived in the United States in May 1898 that Admiral Dewey had destroyed a Spanish fleet at Manila, most Americans had to go to an atlas to find the part of the world in which that city lay. The nation was not prepared for the idea of a six thousand mile expedition into the Orient, and the thought of establishing a colonial possession there was even further removed from consideration. Yet within a year we had not only occupied Manila and driven the Spanish from the Philippines, but we were well on the way toward taking over control of the entire archipelago.

In the fighting with the Filipino insurgents which followed the peace with Spain, it was found essential to hire natives who were familiar with the country to guide the Americans through the dense tropical jungles of the islands. The first of these scout companies was formed from the tribe of Macabebes, traditional enemies of the Tagalogs who were furnishing much of the opposition to American rule. Later, however, most of the "Christian Tribes" were represented in the companies, which by the middle of 1901 counted over thirty in northern Luzon alone. In that year their organization was standardized by act of Congress, and the men were transferred from the status of civilian employees to that of soldiers. In that year, too, they received the designation "Philippine Scouts," under which they rendered valuable service, both to the Army and to their native country.

In 1904 they were clothed in the regulation infantry uniform of khaki breeches, blue shirt, felt campaign hat, and laced leggins. It was not a very attractive dress—indeed this period probably saw the United States uniform reach its lowest ebb. The khaki colored cotton drilling introduced at the time, like so much else in the Spanish conflict, suffered from insufficient planning. The official opinion of one general officer on this subject may be considered typical of the rest of the Army. "The khaki uniforms furnished," he wrote, "are objectionable in every respect. The material is poor and the clothing ill-fitting, badly made, and the original diversities of color are multiplied with every washing. The material . . . is fit neither for campaign nor garrison purposes." It is only fair to say that the uniform was improved greatly later, but it was some years before the Scouts felt the benefit.

The American officer in the plate wears the regulation white duck uniform which, save for the high collar, was so well adapted to the tropics. It could only be worn off duty. Like that worn by the soldier, the "P" on his insignia indicates he is attached to the Philippine Scouts.

In 1901 the Scouts, being small men and required to operate in wooded country, had been issued the short Springfield carbine, firing a black powder cartridge. It was an old-fashioned and none too accurate weapon, and one shot was enough to disclose the position of the firer. But its .45 caliber slug carried a terrific wallop which was more effective in stopping a Moro *juramentado* running *amok* than a whole magazine of modern bullets.

[MS "History of Native Troops in the Philippine Islands" (AGO 317496), and memorandum on uniform of American officers of Philippine Scouts, April 18, 1905 (MSO 1003217), in The National Archives; Division of the Philippines, General Orders No. 183, July 22, 1901; *Report of the Major General Commanding the Army*, 1899, part 3, page 226; James A. LeRoy, *The Americans in the Philippines* (2 vols., Boston, 1914); contemporary photographs.]

Scout in field dress　　　　　　　*Officer in white undress uniform*

PHILIPPINE SCOUTS · 1904

PLATE 27. Staff and Pioneer Infantry, A.E.F., 1918

THE FIRST YEAR of American participation in the World War saw our armies expanded from 200,000 to 4,000,000 men. Half of this number went to France with the American Expeditionary Force. The problems of controlling these masses in the face of modern warfare were gigantic, and it was necessary to adopt, among other expedients, the general staff system then in use by the Allied armies. A staff has been correctly called "the brains of an army"; its officers make it possible for the commander to obtain an accurate and up-to-date picture of conditions and to reach an effective decision. This staff system, developed in the A.E.F., is of the greatest importance today.

The officer in the plate belongs to a division staff as is indicated by his red arm band. He wears two articles which show he is in France: the oversea cap and the Sam Browne belt. Like the staff and so many other features of the A.E.F., these were adopted from the French and the British. On his left side hangs a gas mask, which, with perhaps a map case and the armband that gave him the right of way on crowded roads, about completed his equipment.

The soldier is of the pioneer infantry, a branch of the service whose creation in 1917 suggests the increased complexity of warfare. Actually no one really knew what the pioneers were supposed to do, but the general idea was to have them furnish units who could closely follow an attack, making immediate repairs and installations, all the while being ready to fight if needed. The pioneer in this plate is obviously equipped for this double duty.

He wears the long pack, an arrangement which will be remembered feelingly by many today. A spade has been added to the extra boots, blankets, mess gear, and other things on his back. His fighting equipment includes the rifle (a model 1917 Enfield), bayonet, trench knife, and an extra bandoleer of ammunition. On his chest, in the "alert" position, hangs his gas mask. He is about as "heavy" an infantryman as one could find, but, needless to say, if he got into a scrap, a large part of his dunnage would speedily be tossed to the ground.

Both men wear the olive drab uniform which had by then become standard. A few months later the coats and helmets were enlivened by the addition of divisional insignia, and other concessions were made to appearance, but in the fall of 1918 the Yankee clothing was nothing if not dull. Just as well, perhaps, for most of it stayed covered with mud.

[War Department, "Tables of Organization and Equipment," No. 102, April 20, 1918, and No. 103, July 10, 1918; Special Regulations No. 41, August 15, 1917, and subsequent amendments; A.E.F., General Orders No. 23, August 20, 1917, No. 7, January 9, 1918, No. 134, August 15, 1918; contemporary photographs.]

Lieutenant Colonel of a division staff   *Pioneer in full field kit*

STAFF AND PIONEER INFANTRY, A. E. F. · 1918

PLATE 28. Parachute and Ranger Infantry, 1944

The coming of the Second World War not only increased the strength of American infantry to the greatest point in its history, but it introduced several new and highly specialized types of foot soldier. Of these, the two most spectacular were the paratrooper and the Ranger. Here we see one of each as they looked on D-Day in Normandy.

The primary mission of parachute infantry is to be air transported behind the enemy's main line of resistance, there to drop and employ commando tactics. In this dangerous work they are joined by other infantrymen who land in gliders and by airborne artillery, engineers and the like; all these together go to make up an airborne division.

The first American paratroopers were organized, rather experimentally, in 1940. The next year saw the spectacular German drop on Crete and our own planning for large scale airborne operations took a more vigorous turn, culminating with the creation of the 82d and 101st Airborne Divisions in 1942.

Despite the fact that the paratrooper makes his first critical move by air, once he lands he is an infantryman and has to fight as such for weeks on end. To do both jobs the paratrooper in 1944 wore a two-piece jump suit with immense pockets, and with the trousers tucked into laced leather boots. For some time, early in the war, he alone of all the Army wore these boots and he was ferociously proud of them. But gradually other troops were issued footgear like them and the paratrooper saw this distinction disappear. The jump suit, however, remained his alone; this, his special cap insignia and airborne shoulder sleeve patch served to identify Jo Jump, if such kind of identification was necessary.

While the paratrooper came as a novelty to the Army, the Ranger carried a centuries old proud name, peculiarly in the American tradition. Long before our Revolutionary War the colonies sent out companies of rangers to scout along the frontier and protect the settlements from Indian attack. In the French and Indian War, Robert Rogers and his men established an undying reputation for daring, skill and endurance. Indeed, when the six modern Ranger battalions were formed in 1942, the rules laid down by Rogers for his Ranger companies in 1757 were reprinted and used in the training of the new men.

Like the British Commandos and the U.S. Marine Corps' Raiders, the Rangers were trained to strike fast and hard, deep into hostile country. It was their mission to destroy and demoralize the enemy in every way they could and so hinder his main operations. They saw action on many fronts—in Africa, Sicily, Italy, France, New Guinea and the Philippines. The Rangers normally wore laced leather boots, light equipment, and a knife hung handy for use; otherwise their gear differed in no great degree from that of the other infantry.

[*Army Lineage Book*, II, Infantry; Leonard Rapport and Arthur Northwood, *Rendezvous with Destiny: A History of the 101st Airborne Division* (Washington, 1948); contemporary photographs and descriptions.]

PARACHUTE AND RANGER INFANTRY · 1944

PLATE 29. United States Constabulary, 1950

W HEN, EARLY in 1952, the United States Constabulary was ended and its units merged with the Seventh Army, there passed from the rolls one of the most colorful and efficient organizations of our modern Army. It had been to a considerable extent the product of its first commander, Major General Ernest W. Harmon, the energetic and peppery former commanding general of the 1st and 2d Armored Divisions. Although its life span was less than five years, the impression the Constabulary made upon the war-weary and frightened people of Western Germany will not be forgotten within this generation.

The Constabulary squadrons were formed in 1946 by drawing veteran units from the 1st and 4th Armored Divisions and several separate Cavalry outfits, then on occupation duty in Germany. As the units were transferred to the Constabulary they were renamed but allowed to keep their old numbers. Thus the 10th Armored Infantry Battalion of the 4th Armored Division became the 10th Constabulary Squadron. The new squadrons, however, never lost sight of their own history and honors, and when the Constabulary was broken up in 1952 they reverted to their former names and positions in the Army.

The Constabulary units were given a distinctive uniform: helmet liners with triple stripes of yellow-blue-yellow, shoulder patches with the "thunderbolt" insignia, and yellow nylon scarfs. The men were also authorized to wear full cut blouses, made obsolete by the Eisenhower jacket, and Sam Browne belts, and were the first troops in Europe to receive the dressy cut-down cavalry boot for service wear. Their jeeps, tanks and other vehicles were also marked with the distinctive yellow-blue-yellow stripes, which earned for the Constabulary the nickname of *Kartoffelkäfer*, or potato bug, from the villagers.

These heavily-armed and colorfully uniformed troopers immediately caught the attention of the German populace. Each man was armed with a pistol and either an M-1 rifle or a sub-machine gun. The three-man patrol jeeps all mounted a caliber .30 machine gun and each Constabulary troop was equipped with armored cars carrying 37 millimeter cannon and caliber .50 machine guns. A light tank troop and a horse platoon was stationed at each regimental headquarters. It is interesting to note that while the newspapers in the United States were bewailing the passing of horse cavalry, ten platoons of Constabulary horsemen were guarding the peace and securing the frontiers of Germany.

The motto of the Constabulary was "Mobility, Vigilance, and Justice," and its troopers were picked men, trained to handle both civilians and soldiers under any situation which might arise. The entire force was modeled along the lines of the New York State Police and troopers were taught to be helpful and kind wherever possible, but always firm in the discharge of their duties. Thus was the Constabulary able to give the new generation of Germans hope and a sense of security, and instill in them some of the ideals of democracy.

[MS history by Paul M. Linton, one time Lieutenant, U.S. Constabulary; "A Progress Report on the U.S. Constabulary," in *Military Review*, October 1949; contemporary photographs.]

Officer, 2nd Cavalry, dress uniform   Trooper, field service uniform

UNITED STATES CONSTABULARY · 1950

PLATE 30. 1st Cavalry Division, 1950

No DIVISION is more jealous of its customs and traditions than the 1st Cavalry. For though the Division itself was not formed until 1916, many of its outfits date back to the Civil War and the Indian campaigns of the Old West.

The Division has done all its own fighting in the Pacific and Far East. When its proud old Cavalry regiments were dismounted in 1942 it became a hard-hitting infantry command which specialized in amphibious landings and jungle fighting. Yet the 1st Cavalry Division never gave up the trappings of its earlier days. Not only was the old name preserved (later the word "Infantry" was added in parentheses), but its companies continued to be known as "troops" and their men as "troopers." And the troopers still marched under the red and white guidons of the old horse regiments and wore the yellow insignia of their grandsires.

In the Second World War the Division slugged it out with the Japanese in the Admiralty Islands, on Leyte and on Luzon, where it had the honor of being the first division to reach the city of Manila. Thereafter it served as occupation troops in Japan until called without warning in 1950 to help stem the Red flood pouring into South Korea. On 15 July it boarded British and American ships and sailed, mid the threat of typhoons and Communist attack, across the murky Straits of Shimonoseki. Its troopers were mostly young boys who had never been under fire, yet somehow the spirit of their ancestors—of the grizzled horsemen of the Plains and the tough jungle fighters of the Admiralties, took hold of their hearts and the 1st Cavalry Division entered the bloody battle for South Korea like a veteran outfit. Taking position on the right flank of the United Nations line it relieved the pressure on the hard-pressed dogfaces of the 24th Division who had been holding out so gallantly for the past two weeks.

There was a story current in the Southwest Pacific that if you saw an MP standing up to his waist in mud but with polished shoes and white gloves, you were close to the 1st. Cavalry Division. Tough and rugged when there was need, the troopers could put on as colorful a show as any in the Pacific. Nowadays the three cavalry regiments still wear yellow scarfs on parade, as do the tankers and reconnaissance people. The Division's artillerymen, of course, wear red. But the light blue Infantry scarf is not seen anywhere in the Division.

[E. J. Kahn, Jr. and Henry McLemore, *Fighting Divisions* (Washington, 1945); Department of the Army, *Korea - 1950* (Washington, 1952); contemporary photographs.]

Military Policeman, summer uniform   *Artillery Officer, winter field uniform*

1st CAVALRY DIVISION · 1950

PLATE 31. Women's Army Corps, 1954

ALTHOUGH WOMEN's role in war has normally been outside the ranks of the armed forces, on many occasions in the past they have been counted among the principal actors. Within recent years these activities have increased tremendously. Today women share with men in a large part of the danger and responsibility of conflict.

The most familiar and perhaps the most beloved military duty performed by women is that of the nurse. Female nurses were authorized for the Army as early as 1802, and in the Civil War they proved their worth beyond question. Until 1901 they were considered civilian employees, but in that year the Nurse Corps was formed as part of the military establishment. Since then its members have been as much soldiers as any rifle-carrying doughboy.

Forty years later the demands of the Second World War brought forth another great organization for women, familiarly called the WAC. This Corps was initially established in 1942 as the Women's Army Auxiliary Corps. A year later Congress made it a regular component of the Army and the word "auxiliary" was dropped from the name. In this first year the officers of the Corps wore a distorted version of the American eagle which they fondly dubbed "The Buzzard." In 1943 he was laid aside and they affixed to their caps the eagle worn by all other Army officers.

During the Second World War the WAC enlisted women were given basic training and then specialized instruction as clerks, cooks, bakers and drivers. Others were trained as medical technicians, and as specialists in various technical services. The WAC ran its own Officer Candidate School, graduating a total of sixty classes. At its peak strength the Corps totalled about 100,000 women.

Between 1943 and the end of the war more than 17,000 members of the WAC served overseas—from Bermuda to Ceylon, and from Greenland to the Gold Coast of Africa. Today the Corps is much smaller but more than a third of its women serve overseas. The present day WAC's on active duty are Regulars in the main, but a sizeable part of the Corps consists of Reservists. Thus far the National Guard contains no women of the WAC.

The Corps wears smartly designed service uniforms of a taupe color with tan leather fittings. These are of wool or cotton, depending on the season. A white summer uniform is authorized for dress wear, and "special duty clothing" of several sorts are issued. The two women in the picture wear summer uniforms.

These same uniforms, with different insignia, are worn also by the Army Nurse Corps and by other women of the Army Medical Service. The nurse, however, has one dress not found in the WAC—probably the best known and respected uniform worn by a woman. This is what the Army calls its "uniform, nurses, cotton, white," and any soldier who has occupied a hospital bed will long remember what that uniform has meant to him.

[*Military Laws of the U.S.*, 1929, page 155; *The Army Almanac*; current uniform regulations and photographs.]

NCO, summer service uniform　　　　　*Officer, summer dress uniform*

WOMEN'S ARMY CORPS · 1954

PLATE 32. Army Bands, 1954

It HAS OFTEN been pointed out that ours is not a singing army. Yet the American soldier of today has a broad musical heritage—rich in both songs and music—on which to draw. The story of Army bands is part of that heritage.

Military music has marched with the armies throughout all American history. The Continental soldier heard it from the day at Boston when the regimental fifes and drums began to shrill out *Yankee Doodle*. General Scott's men climbed into their boats at Vera Cruz, in the first great amphibious operation in our history, while the bands aboard the transports played *Hail Columbia* and the *Star Spangled Banner*. Sheridan's mounted bands were stationed just behind his line of battle, playing their liveliest airs; and Custer, on the Plains, often followed the practice by taking the 7th Cavalry band with the regiment, even on winter campaigns. One bitterly cold morning—so cold it was that instruments stuck to the bandsmen's lips—the band played *Garryowen* as the Seventh galloped into a Cheyenne camp.

In more recent wars our bands have, when allowed, taken every bit as active a part as before. We had first to get rid of the idea, however, that the bandsman must serve as a stretcher bearer when the fighting started. It was the British who finally convinced us of the value of keeping our bands intact to play for fighting men, and this the bands did whenever they could.

Traditionally the musician is the gayest dressed soldier of an army and this is as true today as ever. The drum major, as every one knows, is the gayest one of all, and a glance at the drum major of the West Point Band shows he is no exception. His tall feather plume, musician's sword, baldric with its miniature drumsticks, and silver headed baton are historically correct and all date from centuries back. His dark blue coat and lighter blue trousers follow the traditional colors of the Army uniform. This one is his winter full dress; the West Point Band has a variety of other uniforms.

The musician of the Army Band is also in winter full dress. His uniform, gay as it is, differs from the preceding in one marked respect. It is a new uniform, without heritage, designed specifically to furnish a bright patch of color on parade. Not one of its fittings has any history to it or reason for existence other than show.

The third bandsman wears the regular Army summer uniform with a few added features. In this he resembles many other military bands around the country, who have achieved smartness and color by the use of such simple changes in uniform. The winter dress uniform of the First Army Band closely resembles that worn at West Point.

The three units represented here are counted among the famous bands of the country. Their members are serious, skilled instrumentalists. What they can contribute toward the well-being of the troops they play for can never be accurately measured, but assuredly it is considerable. It is altogether fitting that this series end with a note of appreciation to the Army bandsman.

[William C. White, *A History of Military Music in America* (New York, 1944); contemporary photographs and personal observation.]

First Army Band, summer uniform

The Army Band, winter dress uniform   *West Point Band, Drum Major in winter full dress*

ARMY BANDS · 1954

References

DETAILS IN PLATES

PLATE 2, English flintlock lockplate with gooseneck hammer, used early in the Revolution. PLATE 3, Flintlock cavalry or "horse" pistol, period of the Revolution. PLATE 4, Officer's silver laced epaulette, period of the Revolution. PLATE 6, Flintlock lockplate of the U. S. Musket, Model 1808. PLATE 7, Reverse of a flintlock lockplate of the period of the War of 1812. PLATE 8, Pick-and-brush for use with a flintlock musket; tassel to a shako cord. PLATE 12, Percussion lockplate of the U. S. Rifle Musket, Model 1841, one of the earliest percussion types. PLATE 15, Breech mechanism of the U. S. Carbine, Model 1843, showing "North's Improvement" for operating the lock. PLATE 16, Percussion lockplate of the U. S. Rifle Musket, Model 1855, showing the Maynard tape primer. PLATE 22, Brass shoulder "scale" and hat decoration for full dress wear during the Civil War. PLATE 25, U. S. Magazine Carbine, Model 1896, and U. S. Magazine Rifle, Model 1892, the first of our magazine weapons, based on the Krag-Jorgenson system. PLATE 26, Lockplate of the U. S. Carbine, Model 1890, the last of our single-shot breechloaders.

THE HISTORY OF THE ARMY

OLIVER L. SPAULDING, *The United States Army in War and Peace* (New York, 1937)
WILLIAM A. GANOE, *The History of the United States Army* (New York, 1924)
EMORY UPTON, *The Military Policy of the United States* (Washington, 1904)
JOHN DICKINSON, *The Building of an Army* (New York, 1922)

AMERICAN MILITARY DRESS, ARMS AND ACCOUTREMENTS

QUARTERMASTER GENERAL, *The Army of the United States* (New York, 1886)
This first series of forty-four plates by H. A. Ogden appears in several different forms, the one above has a text by Henry Loomis Nelson. To this series three new plates were added in 1901. In 1908 twenty-three additional plates by the same artist were published without text, bringing the coverage through 1907. Up to 1861 the plates must be used with caution, thereafter they are unexcelled.

Dress regulations of the Army.
These have appeared in a wide variety of forms. Until about 1814 they were issued in manuscript, thereafter for many years they were published as General Orders. Until 1881 they also appeared in Army Regulations, but from that date to about 1925 they were usually made the subject of special publications. In recent years the uniform has been specified once more in Army Regulations.

JAMES E. HICKS, *Notes on United States Ordnance* (2 vols., Mt. Vernon, N. Y., 1940)
This valuable work combines the documentary background of our regulation weapons with excellent scale drawings of each type—and the parts of each type—by Andre Jandot.

HAROLD L. PETERSON, *The American Sword, 1775-1945* (New Hope, Pa., 1954)
Detailed and scholarly coverage of all swords carried by American armed forces.